Private L

7 Steps to Earning 1K to 5K per Month Selling Exclusive Products on Amazon FBA for Beginners with Private Labelling

Copyright © 2015

All rights reserved. No part of this book may be reproduced in any form without permission in writing from the author. Reviewers may quote brief passages in reviews.

Disclaimer

No part of this publication may be reproduced or transmitted in any form or by any means, mechanical or electronic, including photocopying or recording, or by any information storage and retrieval system, or transmitted by email without permission in writing from the publisher.

While all attempts and efforts have been made to verify the information held within this publication, neither the author nor the publisher assumes any responsibility for errors, omissions, or opposing interpretations of the content herein.

This book is for entertainment purposes only. The views expressed are those of the author alone, and should not be taken as expert instruction or commands. The reader of this book is responsible for his or her own actions when it comes to reading the book.

Adherence to all applicable laws and regulations, including international, federal, state, and local governing professional licensing, business practices, advertising, and all other aspects of doing business in the US, Canada, or any other jurisdiction is the sole responsibility of the purchaser or reader.

Neither the author nor the publisher assumes any responsibility or liability whatsoever on the behalf of the purchaser or reader of these materials.

Any received slight of any individual or organization is purely unintentional.

Table of Contents

Introduction

Chapter 1 : Understanding Amazon FBA

Chapter 2 : Step 1

Chapter 3 : Step 2

Chapter 4 : Step 3

Chapter 5 : Step 4

Chapter 6 : Step 5

Chapter 7 : Step 6

Chapter 8 : Step 7

Conclusion

Bonus Chapter: What is Passive Income?

Introduction

First and foremost, I want to congratulate and thank you for taking your time to download the book "7 Steps to Earning 1K to 5K per Month Selling Exclusive Products on Amazon FBA for Beginners with Private Labelling."

This book contains seven validated steps and plans that can help you to strategically start and maintain a rich, well oiled online business. Running an Amazon FBA enterprise will automatically yield you 1K to 5K per month by selling exclusive products on Amazon FBA.

A majority of individuals have underestimated the influence of the Amazon FBA. However, this book discloses seven valid steps that can help a beginner make 1K to 5K per month. It only takes a beginner a little time to sell products online.

This book will help you to understand various perspectives that may have been overwhelming when you thought of starting an online business. There are seven steps that have been tested regarding how a newbie can start selling exclusive products on Amazon FBA and make 1K to 5K per month. Thus, you will understand why you should use the Amazon FBA platform while doing business. In addition, you will learn how to establish a new FBA Amazon account, where to acquire profitable inventory for sending to the FBA store, learning the shipping procedures encompassed with Amazon FBA and understand the process of pricing your FBA inventory to be sustainable on Amazon. Additionally, you will learn how to determine the best product to sell on the Amazon FBA and, most importantly, how to acquire consent for selling in the gated categories. Last but not least, you will discover how to mount your enterprise, employ workers, and make goals for future of your business.

This book is the best gift I can give to you. I will show you that you do not need to be an expert in order to build your income. You do not need to have much money to begin this venture. In addition, you do not need to work extremely hard in order to make 1k to 5k per month. All you need to do is make a commitment that you will not surrender; you will endure the hard work and will not stop struggling until you prosper. If you make his commitment prosperity will not be an issue of "IF" for you, but an issue of "WHEN".

Thank you once again for taking time to download this book. I hope it will be of great assistance to you.

Chapter 1

Amazon FBA stands for Fulfilment by Amazon. Unlike numerous other untrusted selling platforms, Amazon FBA takes into consideration various challenges that may halt the advancement of beginners just like you when trying to build a profitable online business. It is important to understand that the majority of people fail to succeed in business because of the time commitment required to maintain the business in progress.

To be very specific, Amazon permits you, the seller, to send entire products and goods you intend to sell on the Amazon platform to their stores, which are located all over the United States.

The moment that products you have sent to the Amazon warehouses and listed online are sold, their employees will locate the item, pack it up and ship it. These workers also handle any customer service issues that require attention, and are responsible for ensuring the satisfaction of the buyer. This allows you as the seller to wait for items to sell without any hassle. Now, do you understand the value of this selling system? It is huge! Can you imagine the time it would take to process 100 orders per day by yourself?

In addition, can you calculate the time it would cost you to find the goods and products you stored away?

It is the responsibility of Amazon to properly maintain all of your products and goods in a very organized way. Amazon ensures the items are stored according to the level of frailness. Therefore, there will be no breakage of your products. In addition, these products to be sold are stored in such a way as to ensure they can be located with ease. This means that Amazon will store entire items you have for sale, and you do not need to worry with organizing them in a storage locker or your house.

Kindly note the Amazon FBA selling platform is the only platform where your products for sale are organized by employees. In other trading platforms, it is your responsibility to organize the item and handle customer issues. You will have to spend a lot of time managing selling and dealing with issues, thus, it would be of great importance for you to make the decision to sell on Amazon.

Unlike other selling platforms, Amazon permits you to control your time and concentrate on sourcing inventory to sell, which is the most important part of any market. The lifeblood of any resale business is the ability to source for these products. In this case, while selling on Amazon you will have all the time you need to source for these products.

Chapter 2

Step 1: Establishing a New Amazon FBA Account

Selling products in Amazon's FBA marketplace is a great way for you to earn some extra cash by working as a personal seller, or to make substantial profits as a recognized online retailer. Lucky for you, taking this golden opportunity is not at all difficult. In fact, Amazon has made the process of becoming an Amazon seller very easy. All you have to do is follow the steps below, which thoroughly explain the way to set up an Amazon selling account.

Case #1 – For those who already own an Amazon Buyer Account:

If you have been making purchases through Amazon or if you have previously bought any kind of goods through Amazon, all you will have to do to set up your Amazon seller account is add the selling goods option to your already existing Amazon account. In order to set up this option, you will need to log in to your Amazon account, and then go to 'Your Account' page. After getting there, find the 'Sell Your Stuff' connection located in the right triangulation and click on it. This link will take you to a button on the 'Sell Your Stuff' page where you will be able to establish a personal account that serves a seller account for users who will be selling a small number of goods. If you are going to sell a large quantity of goods, however, you will have to click on the 'Learn More' button located at the bottom of the page. After doing this, you will be directed to the 'Sell Professionally' information centre. The 'Sell Professionally' account is also known as the 'Pro Merchant' and it costs $39.99 as a monthly fee. This account is aimed at entrepreneurs looking to market and sell a big amount of goods and to create a bigger business through Amazon.

Required Goods and Seller Information:

After you decide which kind of Amazon Selling account you want to start, your next step will be to catalogue your merchandise. You can do this through utilizing the Amazon search button to search for any product by category, name or its ISBN/UPC/ASIN number. The resulting search results will show recommended products. When you see the product, click on the button that says, 'Sell Yours Here'.

Describe the condition of your goods (used or new)

Pricing (Amazon will provide you with the lowest price to be used as a reference)

Quantity of goods for sale

Shipping (you can either ship the product offered yourself or leave it up to Amazon to ship the product using Fulfilment by Amazon)

Shipping periods (standard or expedited)

The following page will ask you to fill out information about your business or yourself if you are selling the product personally. On this page, you will be asked to:

Fill out the business name or your username

Appraise your contact particulars

Authorize the 'Amazon Services Enterprise Solution' Agreements

Give your bank account information (so you can receive payment)

Your phone number is also necessary for Amazon to be able to confirm the information on the file using a personal documentation number.

Case #2 – For those who don't own an Amazon Account:

If you have never made any purchases through Amazon in the past, and do not have an Amazon account, your first step will be to set up an Amazon account. This account will be used to both buy and sell products through Amazon.

First, visit www.AmazonServices.com. Once you are on that page, you will be able to see the 'Learn More' button. Click that button, then select the type of the marketing account that you need, choosing between 'Sell Professionally' and 'Individual Seller' accounts. You will be required to provide Amazon with email address, a password and a business name or business title. The following step will be agreeing to the 'Amazon Services Business Solution Agreements', after which the process will be the same as that described in the first case above. After following these steps, you will have taken the first step towards making money through Amazon!

Chapter 3

Step 2: Important Tips for New Sellers on the Amazon Marketplace

Selecting which products you want to sell may become overwhelming and for good reason. This step is probably the most important one in setting up your Amazon business. However, do not let frustration stop you from chasing success and giving this step enough thought in order to make the right decision. You need not worry, there are many ways to choose great inventory.

Get the Perspective

First of all, you need to know that there is much more to finding inventory to sell on Amazon than just searching for some old "stuff" on eBay. You need to think along the lines of a store; visualize what kind of merchandise you would find while shopping in a store rather than what you would see at a yard sale, for example.

Get Educated

Of course, even with that perspective, there are many possibilities for products that can be sold on Amazon. It will take a little time and practice, but before long you will begin to have an eye to spot profitable items and differentiate the good items from the bad ones. However, we all happen to stumble across profitable merchandise at some point, but making wise buying decisions means you will need to educate yourself a bit. For the most part, product sourcing is going to require research and utilizing your head.

Think for Yourself

You can get a lot of online sellers who may be willing to share that an individual category is the best, or that thrift merchandise sells for the greatest benefit and you must stick with that plan. Maybe you read that others have made a thrilling sell of things they purchased at a local the retail store (Retail Arbitrage). Still others will inform you that getting a few good wholesale items is the perfect way to start. There are so many preferences, and you need to think for yourself and figure out which items and which strategies work best for you. Just because something worked perfectly for others doesn't mean it suits you, and alternately, just because a certain item is not working out well for other sellers doesn't mean it is not a good fit for your individual situation.

You may hear of other sellers who are selling items similar to what you have in mind, and reaping huge rewards. Let this give you hope and determination instead making you feel defeated.

Keep Money in Mind

Jumping in with both feet, spending money on goods, no matter where you acquire them, with little or no education is the worst way to initiate a "Real Enterprise". You need to learn the ropes first, which means you need to acquire items without spending a fortune and with as little stress as possible. Learn while doing, this will help you to learn in a much faster manner. You will also want to consider the number of sellers on Amazon, as well as the pricing of their merchandise.

Get Connected

We can tell you from our experiences that the plan explained above will work. However, all of the above strategies will not work if you do not attack them with a technical know-how. Starting an online business means you will be working closely with technology and that your business will be entirely reliant on it.

You can make the most out of your online business and maximize your profits if you are able to work anywhere and at any time. For that purpose, you will require a smart phone and possibly an app. If you do not own a smartphone, you will need to get one because the phone will be used to "scan" goods. You will be able to learn how to use the computer in order to "test the waters" before you invest in any equipment, services or tools. Find some goods around your home that have barcodes to practice on, and store them on Amazon.com.

If you own a functioning smart phone you will need to acquire an app to start reconnaissance. There are free apps that you can utilize, but we recommend beginning with the app Profit Bandit, which is only $10. This app offers you all of the data you require in one place. If you can't get Profit Bandit, download Amazon's free app, Amazon Price Check, for Android or iPhone. That way, you will be able to work on the go, and turn the time you would normally waste waiting, or commuting into money.

Chapter 4

Step 3: Comprehending Shipping Procedures Encompassed with Amazon FBA

The Shipment Formation Workflow assists you in shipping your merchandise to the Amazon fulfillment centers by utilizing Shipping strategies. A shipping plan is the collection of merchandise that you would like to send to the Amazon fulfillment centers. Building your shipping plan is comprised of choosing the merchandise you need to address, representing the quantity of every product, and marking your products for storage and shipment.

The warehouse is receiving and shipping procedures are concentrated on for distributors and manufacturers. Processes that minimize costs and optimize efficiency contribute importantly to effective business functions in these markets. Receiving, order fulfilment, shipping and inventory control are the basic procedures in the warehouse system. Prosperous warehouse shippers adhere to a few basic regulations to internally regulate procedures.

Receiving

After shipping, the products are derived in the warehousing. The process entails the receipt of raw products or materials, updating inventory annals to demonstrate the new products, and placing the products in their correct place for suitable inventory management and organization. Equipment like pallet and dollies loaders is utilized to unload products from trucks at the loading docks and carry them to their place in inventory storage. This step must be comprised of the use of suitable equipment and safe unloading. Receiving the inventory includes scanning it into the logistics facility software system. Once recorded, there is an easy-to-follow company system that tells the employee where the inventory needs to be place for storage.

Inventory Control

Once the raw goods or materials are received at the warehouse, they arrive at the inventory regulation stage of the warehouse. This starts with suitable storage. At this phase, a forklift is used to transport the inventory and arrange it in the correct position. Companies use computer programs to screen the inventory periodically to avoid shortages or excess. Each product must have a regular degree of model inventory. When the real inventory goes below or above that phase, a message is sent on a computer program to buy current inventory or move old inventory.

Order Fulfilment

Order fulfilment is the procedure triggered by the new customer buying and item, and is completed when the client acquires the item. Order fulfilment tasks include stock warrants, printing invoices, packaging products, retrieving and labelling products, as well as preparing them for shipment. Efficient and suitable communication between employees who receive the order and those who satisfy the order is key in order to fulfil the order swiftly. It is very important to pick the right items from the record, and then package it properly to avoid damage.

Shipping

Shipping is the last step in the record and order fulfilment procedure. At this time, packages must be properly labelled, positioned and packaged for loading and shipment. Shipments must be loaded onto the right automobiles, and then tracked until they reach the client good condition.

Chapter 5

Step 4: The Process of pricing your FBA Inventory to be Sustainable on Amazon

You have found suitable goods, bought them, labelled and shipped them off to Amazon, and now you are pricing the products. At this point, what do you do? You go out and consider more inventory, but how frequently do you plan the prices of the inventory that is sitting in the FBA warehouse? Prices in brick-and-mortar stores vary most of the time, and this is true with Amazon as well. As time passes, your inventory will start gaining and losing to other sellers. Other sellers will possibly begin to undercut your price of the item on sale, while other sellers may start selling out of the product.

Smart sellers take the time to evaluate prices of their products to ensure that they are priced to sell fast and increase profits. Reappraising your inventory on a somewhat regular schedule in order to maintain prices is a wise business choice. As you think about the pricing strategies, you will soon learn that reappraising does not always mean reducing your cost, but could also mean increasing your price.

Now, let us go through how to re-price your products manually. Just click on the pictures located to the right to show a visual representation of every step.

1. Go to Seller Account

2. On the left top of the screen, click on "Inventory."

3. On the sidebar to the left, under "show my inventory," click on the "Active" button. This shows you what products are currently in stock, since there is no need to change something you do not have in stock.

4. The default setting is to classify your inventory, but you can alter what you want to classify in your inventory by date created, product name, quality available, fulfilled by and your price.

5. In this category Amazon offers you with the present low price plus shipping cost for every item, however, you need to be very sensitive to such information. At other times, Amazon will offer you the reduced used price if you are vending a new product. It is always good to open up the personal item's merchandise page to understand for yourself the present price, as well as what the competion is selling that good for, and then deduce for yourself how you need to change the price of your product. A swift click on the ISBN/ASIN link will redirect you the Amazon item page where you can acquire the information you need to price astutely. If you see the little check spot in the "Low Price" pillar, that implies that you have the present lowest price.

6. If you are looking to change the price of a particular item, you can hunt for that product in the search bar situated near the left of the screen. You may search by item name, ASIN, ISBN or SKU.

7. Under the "Your Price" column, you will see the box where you may update prices of the product. Just type in the current price you need. The price box turns into the yellow shaded box. It indicates that you will have an updated price, but you have not updated it on Amazon yet.

8. Submit the new prices to Amazon. You may either do the hard yield in the price box, or you may wait until you are completely done updating the prices for chosen items on that page, and then click on the "Save" button situated at the top of the screen. Once presented, it takes a few moments for Amazon to update the prices for your products.

Now you are equipped with the skills to reappraise your Amazon inventory. Keeping your prices updated and competitive is a main component to a profitable and successful Amazon enterprise.

Chapter 6

Step 5: Determining the best Product to Sell on the Amazon Marketplace.

If you are looking for ideas on how to earn extra cash by selling on Amazon, pay attention to what I am about to tell you. This information will assist you in increasing your benefits and is very good for newcomers. Selling on Amazon allows seller's access to millions of customers looking for items on the website. The Amazon online marketplace allows you to build your business or to just send a few items. Some would like to make this their full-time job, while for others this is more of a part time job. This allows you to vend your wares all over the world. Additionally, you can list your items in over twenty categories.

Online business is the future of entire types of commercial sectors. Numerous organizations and individuals have earned millions by building enterprises online. You may be speculating what these individuals are selling and what you must sell to earn decent cash through an online enterprise. Typically, there needs to be thorough research done on all specific niches. Research on the competition, product demand and traffic volume play a vital role in choosing the best types products. In this chapter, I will make the procedure a little simpler and explain to you how you would select the best types of items to sell online.

Private Label Right items:

Private Label Rights, also referred to as PLR, are one of the easiest and best kinds of online items. PLR simply means that you may claim all rights to the items. You can list a ready to sell item as your product. You only need to buy the item once and can then sell it at your price. Best of all, such products are digital items, so you don't have to worry about delivery and shipping. Customers can simply download when they complete the purchase of the product.

Master Resale Rights of Products:

The Master Resale Rights of products, also known as MRR, are the second best kind that I could recommend to vend online. MRR items are similar as the PLR items, with a few exceptions. You cannot list MRR items as your products. You must keep the owners' information intact. Although you cannot change an items copyright, you can select your price to vend MRR items. These items come with a prepared site and sales letter.

Now I will explain to you why MRR and PLR products make the two best online items. These items are available in most niches that really bring money. Professionals make MRR and PLR products in particular niches where cash flows in endlessly. Furthermore, product creators have years of experience and professional skills, so the product quality you get is exceptional. If you understand how to advertise your website after this is done, MRR and PLR products are the perfect types of items to sell online. You may also get to acquire hundreds of MRR and PLR products completely free by calling free giveaway events. These giveaway events are held several times a year and are available by invitation only. Get free summons to on-going Amazon Internet Marketing Giveaways.

Chapter 7

Step 6: Acquiring Consent for selling in the Gated Group

Selling licensed collegiate and professional team apparel is a tremendous market, with sports fans all over the world buying soft items and hard-line products to support their favorite players and teams. With several knock-offs being found in the market, getting consent for professionally selling the product line is becoming increasingly hard. According to the 2011 New York Times Journal, "The NFL is Squeezing Discounters over Apparel." Consent to sell in the gated community is easier to attain than getting permission to sell soft products like jerseys and hats. You will be required to prove your ability to sell high amounts of products before getting consent. The following steps are viable for getting the consent for selling into the gated community.

Step 1

Check with the collegiate and professional leagues concerning the minimum purchase ethics you should meet to acquire and maintain an agreement to sell licensed items. For instance, the National Football League grants permission to the online retailers who buy more than $3 million in the licensed products from them every year. The Collegiate Licensing can present you with the information for numerous college teams.

Step 2

You need to contact the licensing section of the key sports leagues or your favorite collegiate group. Information is available on the NFL, National Basketball Association and League Baseball Association sites. Ask to speak with a representative in regards to becoming a licensed item vendor in the gated community.

Step 3

At this point, you need to write a formal appeal to vend official team apparel, explaining your location and market. While your focal point might be apparel, do not forget hard-line products that can escalate your bottom line or might be a chance to demonstrate how effective your market is for licensed team items. Send the request to the licensing group of you is attentive in. League representatives refer you to the producers who have licenses for the gated communities and hard-line products.

Step 4

Offer your business strategies and any other pertinent information to the gated group representative upon the appeal. This is a multibillion-dollar business and you need consent to get started, therefore, be honest and upfront about every aspect of your enterprise. Ensure your business plan includes market research of what groups are most general in your area, offering you an ample chance to vend a large amount of hats, jerseys and other team apparel.

Step 5

Finally, you need to negotiate a contract with the gated group representatives. You might have a limited item line agreement with probationary time to ensure you have a good market. The contract can limit you to one team's consent or only allow hard-line items until you can show success. Conduct your business well, and requests for an expanded line are warranted in the amazon gated groups.

Chapter 8

Step 7: Mounting your Enterprise, Employing Workers, and making Goals for the

Future of the Business

The point of this book is to steer your actions and thinking toward sustaining and creating your business. Managerial mentors and their people are asked to explore how actions, behavioral standards and values can assist organizational success.

Values Drive Behavior

A well-used adage in the organizational behavior thought declares that *values* finally drive our *behavior*. In a nut shell, values exert effects over our attitudes while the attitudes influence our behavior. Values are integral to attitude creation and to how we reply to situations and people. Extensive literature is available, dealing with how values standards associate with effective managerial leaderships. An appraisal of this work explains to you with the clear explanation that values are a main component of operative successful leadership. There appears to be a subset of worthy values that support ethical behavior. These core virtuous values influence ethical behavior and seem to have a universal appeal. My version of such values as they apply to ethics is as follows.

Knowledge and Wisdom: The ability to take news and change it to useful material. Wisdom comes from expounding on one's knowledge to interpret information in a manner to make wise decisions. A precondition to doing the correct thing, which means when presented with an ethical dilemma, understanding the difference between right and wrong.

Self-Control: The ability to avoid unethical temptations in business. The ability to take ethical paths needs a pledge to the standards of acting with abstinence. Ethical people articulate "no" to personal gain if it is unpredictable with organizational goodwill and benefit.

Fair Guidance and Justice: This is the fair treatment of individuals regardless of whether they are customers or employees. Justice is served when persons perceive that they get a fair benefit for the effort and energy needed. For instance, a leader's promise to justice is verified repeatedly with the organizational resources allocation. Are certain persons and groups given special care without the regard to objective standards by which to critic fairness? Ethical leaders embrace and value fair guidance and advice.

Transcendence: The realization that there are other things beyond oneself, which are more powerful and permanent than the person. Without these standards, one might tend to be self-absorbed. Leaders who are inspired predominately by the self-interest and exercises of personal influence have restricted authenticity and effectiveness and their business does not succeed.

Kindness and Love: The expression through deeds and words of kindness and love. Researchers have recognized that there seem to be different kinds of "love." In the organizational setting, love refers to the intense positive response to other co-workers, situations or groups. An organization with heart allows for expression, kindness and compassion among people, the goodwill that can be fraught upon when one experiences ethical dilemma.

Integrity and Courage: The courage to perform duties ethically and with integrity. These values comprise differentiating right from wrong and behaving accordingly. They compel one to repeatedly do the right thing without concern for individual results, even when it is not simple.

In practice, the six categories of righteous values explained above are tangled. For instance, the ability to administer resources honestly and offer fair direction to stakeholders together with the way it is maintained by integrity and courage. Difficult decisions neighboring the allocation of limited resources leave some persons and clusters with less than they could expect. The redeeming point is the insight that such choices are made with integrity and fairness. Unpopular choices are simpler to make when they appear to be derived honestly and with integrity.

Ideally, managerial frontrunners and their individuals will act ethically as an outcome of their internalized righteous core standards. I like to think about this as ethics from the inside out. Depending entirely on this inside out perspective, however, is simply inexperienced in several circumstances.

Established behavioral standards and the written ethical codes of conduct can assist in bolstering virtuous standards and endorsing ethical organizational behavior. Behavioral values usually incorporate certain guidelines for behavior within a specific functional workplace. For instance, a sales group might clearly outline the criteria for expense compensation.

Employing the right worker for the right job symbolizes success. Therefore, you must consider the type of work you need done. In this case, if the work requires a professional in a particular field, why should you go for a newbie? In the end, it will mean that the specialists will deliver while the newbies getting experience in your work will fail miserably. There is no shortcut in employment for success. On the other hand, if the work to be completed is a manual job for everyone, you do not need to hire a specialist since it would turn out to be expensive. You just need a normal worker with some small amount of experience.

When you start a business, you must have some objectives and aims that you need established. In this case, it means that those are the goals you need to achieve at the end of the day. Therefore, it is important to remain focused on the goals you need established and do not procrastinate. Do not keep changing your goals. You need to set SMART goals that you are sure you will establish at the end of the day. There is no need to start a business if there are no goals to achieve. This will imply that you will use your money and get no profit. This should not be the case at all. Just set smart, measurable, achievable, realistic and timely goals for your business, and you will never regret being a member of Amazon.

Conclusion

In summary, it is my great hope that downloading the book "7 Steps to Earning 1K to 5K per Month Selling Exclusive Products on Amazon FBA for Beginners with Private Labelling" was rewarding for you. Nothing is for vain, you must have gotten the few points that you wanted to solidify. Particularly, the validated seven steps and plans that can help you strategically start and build a rich oiled-well. It is confirmed that running an Amazon FBA enterprise will automatically yield you 1K to 5K per month by selling exclusive products on Amazon.

Bonus Chapter: What Is Passive Income?

I bet it has never been part of your plan to work for 15,484,125 hours a week just to earn an income that can't even support your mortgage. You wake up at 5:00 o'clock in the morning to prepare for a full-time job where you have to stay for 8 hours in a cramped office, bear with the attitude of your boss and co-workers while hoping that you will win at lottery. You don't even have enough time anymore for your loved ones and you keep on declining their invitations for a night-out.

When you were 15 years old, you dreamt of cruising through the Mediterranean and you're nowhere near prepared for the reality of not being able to set a foot out of the city you're working at. You're nowhere near prepared for the reality of lying face down on your bed after an exhausting day only to wake up five hours later to do the same thing over and over again.

At night, you get nightmares about what will happen after you retire. Will you have enough money to spend while you breathe out the remaining years of your life? Can you even afford buying take-out steaks from the nearest restaurants? You don't want to hassle your children and ask them to take care of your financial needs but perhaps you'll have to prepare a speech begging for assistance just in case.

You consider yourself a really hard-working person and should be considered for sainthood because of it. Your name and face might as well be added next to the word *industrious* in the dictionary. But at the end of the day, it's still not enough. The economy is screwing with you. The minimum wage is killing you. You can't count the number of times you've gotten sick because you live to work and not the other way around.

So you ask if it is possible to earn money without breaking your back and sweating blood. It has always been the teaching of your great-great-great-grandfather to work hard in order to succeed, to dedicate all your hours to making your money grow. Yet you wonder: *Can you actually earn unbelievable amount of profits without the kind of effort that's turning you into a glorified mule?* The answer is a big fat YES. And that is passive income.

Passive income is basically defined as any money that goes into your bank account while you're sipping Virgin on the Rocks on some beach in the Caribbean. It is revenue that you earn even when you aren't really actively working. However, the degree to which you can call working as passive or active varies depending on a person. What may be my definition of passive may be another person's passive.

Our society doesn't really put that much appreciation and emphasis on earning passive income since it has been the common set-up to work for 50 years and retire from any work where we earn active income.

For your information, there are three main types of income namely: active income, passive income, and portfolio income. Active income is your common idea of earnings. It refers to the profits that you worked for. Your salary, for example, as well as the commission and bonus that you receive, are active income. You obtained them after performing labor and services.

The issue with active income is its limitations. One day has only 24 hours and you can't possibly work during those 24 hours. This means that, during the time you aren't working, you're not earning anything. Moreover, active income will cease in cases when you are fired from work or simply cannot perform your job description because of certain reasons.

On the other hand, passive income can go on for the rest of your life. It doesn't take into consideration what you earned from actively participating in business ventures and the wages that you get from it. It also doesn't include the income acquired from interest and dividends from stocks or bonds as they belong to your portfolio income. Direct involvement is not required.

Common business streams where you can earn passive income includerenting your properties, publishing a book, and monetizing your blog. In renting out a space, you are not working 24/7 but by the end of the month, your pocket is heavier. When you publish a book, you get the royalties and a share of the sales whenever someone buys it from a store or download it online. By adding advertisements in your blog, all you have to do is run it and attract traffic and you can already collect revenue from that.

Passive income has two basic categories: residual income and leveraged income. The former is your earnings that occur repeatedly and over time from a work finished. An example of residual income would be a photographer who takes pictures and makes them available for paid downloading and he gets royalty whenever someone downloads one of his pictures. An author who sells an eBook gains residual income whenever someone buys it online.

There are multiple streams where you can generate residual income and the level of involvement in your part depends on the kind of business it is. In online selling, you don't have to get in touch with each of your customers since the buying and selling of online products are automated and facilitated by technology. This provides you with greater freedom to exercise other activities and agendas while your business is running in the background even without your presence.

Meanwhile, leveraged income takes into consideration the participation of other people who will be responsible in creating profits for you. Network marketing is a good example of a source of leveraged income. A network marketer who has a downline usually receives commissions from the sales made by the agents who belong in his downline. In this case, it is the effort and labor of his agents that puts money in his wallet.

Earning passive income is quite different from what we usually imagine as work. Now, there is no need to wake up at the crack of dawn and stumble your way through your bathroom to take a shower and suffocate yourself with your formal business tie. Passive income can be the answer to your dreams. Even by working less, you can earn more and your nightmares about your retirement are solved. It provides you with more personal and financial freedom.

With a sustainable passive income, you can do a lot more things. For one, you can be in a business of your own choosing. Nowadays, the field where we are working at isn't our ideal one. We are forced to settle to be an office staff because it's the position with the vacancy. With passive income, if your passion lies on exercising and physical activities, you can gain income from that by creating work-out manuals and videos and selling them.

Furthermore, if you have multiple business streams that can provide you with the necessary budget for your household, you can opt to find another daytime and stable job which may pay less but is more interesting. Actually, the tool to amassing wealth is through building various and multiple passive income streams. You don't have to worry about the finances because the passive income from your other streams can take care of that for you. Most importantly, you can spend your free hours pursuing your hobbies and staying with your family and re-establishing social relationships that you have neglected before because of too much working.

Printed in Great Britain
by Amazon.co.uk, Ltd.,
Marston Gate.